Dedicated To:
My Raytown Staff & All Teachers

ritten by: Abigail Gartland

I was born on January 6, 1412 in France!

When I was a little girl, I started to hear the voice of St. Michael.

St. Michael told me that there was a big war going on!

He said that God asked me to lead the French people in battle!

I was a little nervous, but knew that God would save me from any danger.

God will always keep me safe, no matter what!

As soon as I heard about this, I went to the castle to tell the king.

When I told the king, he sent me away, but eventually he believed me.

Once he gave the approval, we went into battle, and won!

When I was in battle, I was never afraid!

I said "I am not afraid – for God is with me. I was born for this."

I always trusted that God would keep His word, and keep me safe!

I am the patron saint of France and soldiers.

Do you want to be more like me?

You can celebrate my feast day with me on May 30th!

Whenever you may be afraid, just remember that God is always with you!

Dear Jesus, Thank you for keeping me safe. I love you! Amen.

I pray for you every day of your life.

St. Joan of Arc, pray for us!

pyright:

art: © PentoolPixie
nsed purchased: 1/10/2024

About the Author

Abigail Gartland

I love the saints and I love my faith. The idea for sharing the stories of the saints with little ones came when my dear friend were expecting their first baby. I wanted to create something as unique and special as our friendship. Each book is dedicated to very special people and groups who have enriched my faith in different ways. I am blessed to write these stories and appreciate the unending support of my family and friends. When I am not writing, am a middle school teacher. I hope you enjoy these stories. I pray for each and every person who opens one of my books to learn more about the saints.

Abbie

www.ingramcontent.com/pod-product-compliance
Lightning Source LLC
LaVergne TN
LVHW061632070526
838199LV00071B/6654